Put Beginning Readers on the Right Track with ALL ABOARD READING™

The All Aboard Reading series is especially for beginning readers. Written by noted authors and illustrated in full color, these are books that children really and truly *want* to read—books to excite their imagination, tickle their funny bone, expand their interests, and support their feelings. With five different reading levels, All Aboard Reading lets you choose which books are most appropriate for your children and their growing abilities.

Picture Readers—for Ages 3 to 6

Picture Readers have super-simple texts, with many nouns appearing as rebus pictures. At the end of each book are 24 flash cards—on one side is the rebus picture; on the other side is the written-out word.

Pre-Level 1—for Ages 4 to 6

First Friends, First Readers have a super-simple text starring lovable recurring characters. Each book features two easy stories that will hold the attention of even the youngest reader while promoting an early sense of accomplishment.

Level 1—for Preschool through First-Grade Children

Level 1 books have very few lines per page, very large type, easy words, lots of repetition, and pictures with visual "cues" to help children figure out the words on the page.

Level 2—for First-Grade to Third-Grade Children

Level 2 books are printed in slightly smaller type than Level 1 books. The stories are more complex, but there is still lots of repetition in the text, and many pictures. The sentences are quite simple and are broken up into short lines to make reading easier.

Level 3—for Second-Grade through Third-Grade Children

Level 3 books have considerably longer texts, harder words, and more complicated sentences.

All Aboard for happy reading!

For Reo Savage Kimura, brave cub—P. P.

To Barry (my favorite "bear"), for helping
fulfill my New Mexico dream—Neecy

Text copyright © 2001 by Pamela Pollack. Illustrations copyright © 2001 by Neecy Twinem.
All rights reserved. Published by Grosset & Dunlap, a division of Penguin Putnam Books
for Young Readers, New York. GROSSET & DUNLAP and ALL ABOARD READING are
trademarks of Penguin Putnam Inc. Published simultaneously in Canada. Printed in the U.S.A.

Library of Congress Cataloging-in-Publication Data is available.

ISBN 0-448-42614-5 (GB) A B C D E F G H I J

ISBN 0-448-42523-8 (pb) A B C D E F G H I J

ALL
ABOARD
READING™

Level 2

Bear Cub

By Pam Pollack and Meg Belviso
Illustrated by Neecy Twinem

Grosset & Dunlap • New York

Deep in the hillside,

under a blanket of snow,

a brown bear is sleeping.

She will sleep in her den

until the spring.

Her two cubs are with her.

They were born two weeks ago.

The cubs drink their mother's rich milk.

The bigger cub gets the milk first.

Now they are only the size of gerbils.

But they may grow to be
almost nine feet tall
and may weigh up to 700 pounds.
Brown bears are the largest animals
in North America.

Spring has come.

The bigger cub is the first to follow

his mother out of the den.

The three bears must find food quickly.
The mother bear has not eaten
for six months.

The mother bear

lifts her nose in the air.

She waves her large head

back and forth.

She is sniffing the air for food.

The bigger cub lifts his nose, too.

He is copying his mother.

The smaller cub waves his head

back and forth so hard that

he falls over!

The mother bear remembers a place
where there are lots of roots.
She climbs up the hillside.

The smaller cub is busy

digging in the snow.

His mother grunts.

Then she cuffs him with her paw.

He must pay attention to her.

Baby bears need to learn many things.

Soon the family is eating lots of roots.

The bear cubs now know

where the roots are.

They will not forget.

Every day the bears search for food.

When they are not eating,

the bear cubs play.

They pretend to fight

and run away from danger.

They are learning to take care

of themselves.

Suddenly the mother bear grunts.

The cubs run to her.

The mother bear senses danger—

real danger.

It is another bear.

He roars and rises up

on his hind legs.

He is a lot bigger than

the mother bear.

He is a danger to the cubs.

The mother bear sweeps the cubs

into the bushes.

Now the mother bear charges.

She waves her claws.

She snaps her teeth.

She bellows.

She will do anything to keep him

from her cubs.

The huge bear backs down.

He has learned not to fight

an angry mother bear.

One afternoon in summer,

the bears reach the stream.

It is full of fish.

Other bears are catching fish too.

There is plenty for all.

Bears do not live in packs like wolves.

Grown-up bears usually do not like

to be around other bears.

But at this stream,

they have learned to share.

Each bear has its own way of fishing.

The mother bear holds her breath

and puts her head in the water.

She sees a fish and rushes at it
with her mouth wide open.
The bear cubs copy their mother.
Often they do not catch a fish.
But they are learning.

The bears also find time to play.

They go up a hill

that still has snow.

They paddle at the snow

with their paws.

Soon they begin to slide.

Faster and faster

down the hill they go!

Splash!

They hit the water.

Then they climb out.

They go back up the hill

and do it all over again.

This time they go down backwards!

Soon it is time to look

for a place to sleep.

But wait!

Now there are three cubs!

The third cub has no mother.

No one knows what happened to her.

The little cub needs a mother.

She will not go away.

She cries for food.

The mother bear takes her into the family.

The little bear cub will not be alone again.

At the end of the summer,

the cubs are much bigger.

Now they are about 60 pounds.

When fall comes,

they do nothing but eat.

Imagine if you ate 84 hamburgers a day.

That's how much the mother bear eats.

The bears need to put on lots of weight.

They do not eat at all

during their long winter sleep.

The cubs help their mother make a den.

It is just big enough to fit

all four of them.

In winter, the den will be covered with snow.

The snow protects the den.

It keeps the den warm inside.

The bears will sleep for six months!

Then they will wake up and feel fine.

They won't even be stiff from staying

curled up for so long.

How do they do it?

It is a mystery!

The next year, the bear cubs

know what to do.

They sniff the air for the smell of food.

An old elk is nearby.

It cannot run away from the bears.

The elk lowers its antlers.

The mother bear pushes the cubs aside.

The elk charges.

It catches the mother bear

with an antler.

The mother bear falls down.

Suddenly the biggest cub

rushes at the elk.

He pulls it to the ground.

The mother bear kills the elk.

There is lots of meat to eat.

The bears eat some now

and bury the rest.

Another bear smells the meat.

He wants to dig it up.

That is a big mistake.

The mother bear roars
and stands up on her hind legs.
Beside her are the cubs,
waving their claws.

They have learned to fight.

All the other bear gets is a torn ear

and a scratch

on his back.

The bear cubs are yearlings now.

They do not have to be

with their mother all the time.

Sometimes the cubs explore the woods

all night by themselves.

The biggest cub remembers

fishing from last year.

He is eager to get back

to the stream.

He fishes with his family.

That night, the four bears

go to sleep together.

In another year or two,

they will all go their own ways.

Later on, the bears will have

cubs of their own.

But for now, they are a family.